Life Skills for Smart Young Adults

Smart Young Adult Basic Life Skills

E. Atchley

Table of Contents

Introduction

The life of a young adult is exciting, exhilarating, and full of endless surprises. As you transition from student to adult, you already know that some of those surprises can come along with plenty of stress.

From the moment of college graduation, many young adults already find themselves in debt. In fact, the average bachelor's degree-seeking student takes out upwards of $30,000 in loans (Hanson, 2023).

On top of this, almost one in four Americans between the ages of 18 and 29 are 90 days past due on their credit card debt (Turner, 2023).

These statistics show that it's clear our school system is failing students and not setting them up for success. When young adults are failing to find financial freedom, what does that mean for our future as a whole?

There's no shame in having debt, and for some people, it's exactly what's needed to help propel education or make important purchases. However, when we find ourselves in massive debt, it's harder to save money and prepare for bigger purchases in life, such as cars or houses. Many of us have heard of credit before, and you might have a basic understanding. However, right now, you might be wondering:

- What *really* is credit? Why is it so important to have good credit?

- How can I save money, even if I don't have a lot? How can I do this while still being able to enjoy life?

- What are the most important things to know about financial literacy?

Parents are the biggest influence on personal finance habits for one in three young adults (*Study*, 2023). On top of this, one in four young adults feels like there's no one they can turn to for financial advice (Turner, 2023).

Knowing how to be financially smart doesn't require extensive financial knowledge. With the right tips and tricks, financial literacy is possible for someone who doesn't even understand the basics. That's where I come in! I want to help empower the youth of tomorrow so you can thrive as you navigate through life's ups and downs.

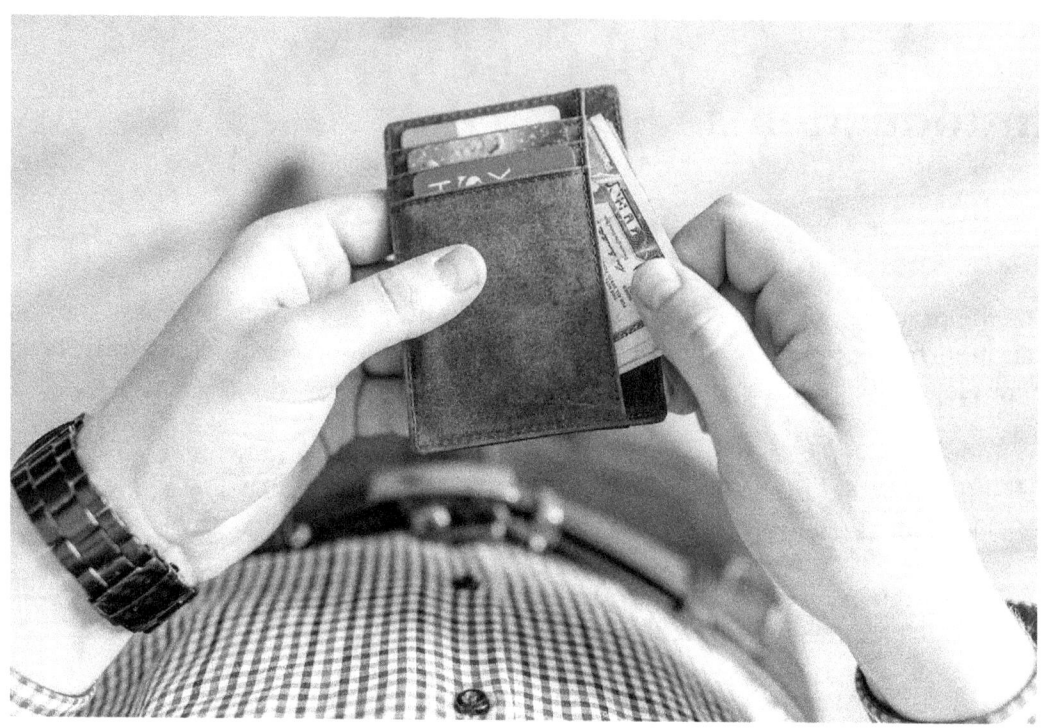

It's essential to set yourself up for success early on, as it can be incredibly hard to dig yourself out of debt once you do fall into it. Between interest rates and annual fees, once you get caught up, it can feel like you are right back at the starting point as debt adds up faster than your savings might.

I'm someone who knows the importance of saving money and living life comfortably within my means. I want young adults to know how and why to do this before it's too late, so they don't have to struggle with debt. Throughout this book, I've provided essential financial insights paired with crucial skills to set you up for financial empowerment. What life throws our way is unpredictable, and there's no telling what might impact our future. The best way to be prepared for whatever may lie ahead is by learning these smart young adult basic life skills!

Chapter 1:

Setting Up Your Future for Success

Why is it important to set yourself up for financial success in the first place?

In 2020, only three in five Americans could cover an emergency that cost $400 (Payne, 2023). This shows us that though the median balance for a savings account in an American household is over $5,000, not many are prepared for the unexpected (Payne, 2023).

Furthermore, only two in five Americans could cover a $1,000 emergency (Renter, 2023).

There's no way of knowing what might happen in the future. Job loss is never something we can plan for, and can occur in even the most high-demand career fields. Even when you're in a position where you could quickly find another job after losing one, we never know if we are going to experience something that could make us unable to work. Car accidents, sicknesses, and other emergencies can cause us to have to walk away from high forms of income, often at no fault of our own.

Being prepared for whatever lies ahead will give you the financial freedom you deserve to live a life of comfort, and even luxury.

The Importance of Financial Literacy

Knowing how to handle money is a skill we need all our lives. Take a moment to assess your current financial situation. Do you feel confident with the money you have? Do you feel secure with the knowledge you have? How much money do you have in your bank account? Do you have a checking account and a savings account? Answering these questions can help you gain an understanding of where you fit into the financial world. Seven in ten millennials are living paycheck to paycheck (*Financial Literacy*, 2023). What this means is that they don't have much in savings, and run out of money a little before their next payday. This can be a stressful life to live, because what if there's an issue with that paycheck? What if they get sick, but don't have paid sick days?

Money might not buy happiness, but it can alleviate stress. Knowing how to stay on top of finances is the most surefire way to stay one step ahead of whatever the unexpected future holds. There's no way of knowing what lies ahead, so staying financially prepared ensures we can handle the many things life throws our way.

Financial literacy will also help us make decisions going forward. As you start to make more money and creep toward those bigger life purchases, it's crucial that you have a good head on your shoulders to know what your options are, and which option is best to take—now, and in the future.

How Debt Builds Over Time

Debt refers to any money that is borrowed with an expectancy to be paid off over time. Examples of types of debt include the following:

- credit cards taken out through banks, major credit card companies, or stores

- loans, such as student, business, or car

- mortgages, which are loans for the acquisition of real estate (like houses)

- unpaid medical bills from hospital visits or other procedures

When acquiring debt, there is usually an established payback plan before the debt is granted. For example, if you sign up for a credit card, you will be given an amount you are approved for and an interest rate on top of this amount.

Interest is the price that is paid for borrowing this debt. Some interest rates can be low, like 5%. Others can be very high, up to 25% or 30%. The interest is usually based on many factors, like your credit history or income amount. I'll get into these details a little later, but for now, I want to provide you with a brief overview of debt so you can gain an understanding of how easy it is for debt to quickly grow over time.

At first, small debt doesn't seem like a big deal. You might take out a credit card with a limit of $300. That doesn't seem like all that much, especially if your weekly or biweekly paycheck is more than that. When you first go to school, taking out a $5,000 loan to cover the semester might not seem like a ton. You're getting a degree that will hopefully help you make $50,000 or more a year, so why not take out a little extra so you can use the additional money on personal expenses?

The thing is, this can quickly build into massive debt if you are not careful—especially with that mindset. If you take out $5,000 per semester, by the end of your four-year education, you're $40,000 in debt. If the interest rate is high, you might end up paying double that by the time you're finally able to pay off those loans. If you take out five different credit cards all with a $300 limit, you're racking up debt in the thousands, which, again, if doubled, can be over $3,000 by the time you pay it off.

Debt isn't something to be scared about, as many of us will rely on it to make important purchases in our lives, like houses or cars. However, if we go into it with the wrong mindset, it can quickly build into something that is no longer manageable. Interest rates seem like low amounts at first, but you don't realize just how intense they are until after you've started to gain a lot of interest on your debt. Taking out more debt is an immediate solution with long-term consequences, so it's best to know what you're getting into before you add onto it.

Finding the Right Job

The best way to increase your budget, money, and income is through the use of a good job. A good job should have the following features.

- Desirable income: This should ensure that you are making enough to cover your bills. While sometimes a low-paying job or an unpaid internship might seem like a good idea, are you still going to be able to make the minimum payments on your bills?

- Additional benefits: Are you gaining other things from this job besides a paycheck? This includes benefits like health insurance, or learning experiences that will help you in your career.

- Reasonable expectations: Are you reasonably able to fulfill the expectations of this job? Can you work the demanding hours set forth? Will you be able to pay your taxes if taxes aren't automatically withdrawn from your paycheck? While some high-paying jobs can be enticing, it's also important to ensure you can reasonably maintain that job.

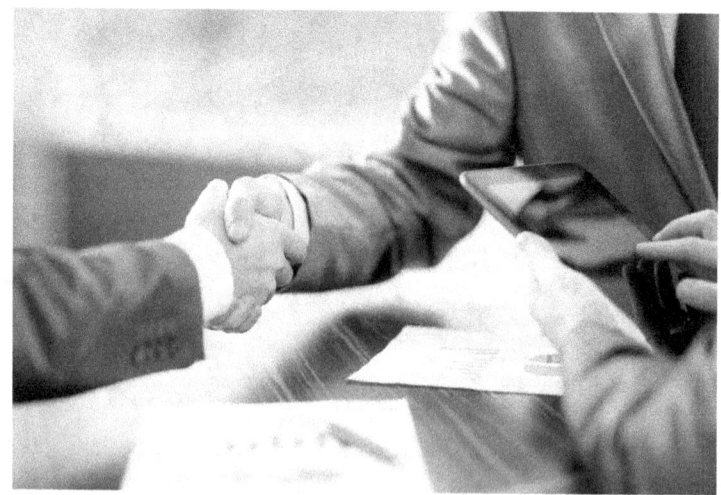

Once you find a position you think you'll excel in, it's then time to land the interview! Below are a few interview tips to ensure you get the position:

- Research the company before your interview. Look at how it started, what its mission statement is, and what some of the employees who work for the company have to say. This will show your passion and intrigue for the job.

- Prepare some responses to questions the night before. Depending on the position, do some research on common interview questions. In general, you will likely be asked things like: Why should I pick you for this job? What are your strengths and weaknesses? What is a time in the past that you were able to demonstrate your skills?

- Come up with some questions of your own for the interviewer. They will likely ask you at the end of the interview if you have any questions. This is your chance to get to know a little more about the position while showing them that you are dedicated and interested.

Getting a job is exciting, but it can also be stressful. Keeping up with a position, especially if you are in college, can be very demanding and overwhelming. Below are some tips to help you maintain your job once you get one:

- Set aside a portion of each paycheck to start savings. It doesn't have to be a ton! Even just $5 a paycheck can be helpful in the future.

- Always show up on time. Even if you are struggling with some of the tasks or demands of the job, showing up on time is a surefire way to show that you are dedicated and passionate about the position.

- Keep your resume updated. Add on new skills as you learn them, and make connections through this job. You never know when it will be time to find the next, higher-paying position.

When all of your friends are hanging out or you just want to stay up to finish watching your favorite series, it can be tempting to call in sick to work or skip out on the job. However, commitment and dedication are among some of the most important qualities to show in your career. Once you find a solid position, do your best to maintain it to help contribute to a brighter future.

Ideas for Additional Income

Sometimes finding a steady job just isn't an option. Whether you have a chaotic schedule or you need to travel frequently, you might not be able to dedicate yourself to a full-time position. That's okay! There are plenty of ways to earn additional income outside of your job. This is also a great way to supplement your income if you are not making enough from a part-time position or internship. Below are some ways you can make additional income to help boost your budget.

- Freelance work: Freelancing involves completing tasks on a per-project basis, usually done through larger companies or individuals where you sign a contract promising the completion of work. As an independent contractor, you have the ability to showcase your talents while working on your own terms. Freelance work often includes creative work like writing, photography, or video editing. You might also be able to showcase your graphic design skills by creating logos, newsletters, and other material for businesses. Fine-tune whatever skills you already have, or familiarize yourself with popular editing software to help boost your freelance business.

- Start a small business: Aside from freelance work, you might even consider starting your own business online. Are you a craftsman who likes to repurpose old furniture? Are you a graphic designer who creates templates for planners or schedules? Do you have an eye for fashion and enjoy sewing or crocheting? If you have any special skills or a craft you enjoy doing, starting your own business is a great way to make money doing something you enjoy.

- Rideshare gigs: If you have a car or a bike, you can make money! There are many apps where you can drive people around or deliver takeout and groceries. You can sign up for multiple different platforms to find the one you like, and if you do a good job, you might even get an occasional big tip from time to time!

- Service positions: Aside from freelance work or starting your own business, there are plenty of flexible career options out there. You might consider dog walking, babysitting, or housesitting as a way to earn extra income.

Don't be discouraged if you're not making a ton of money when you start these side hustles. You will gain more experience, and therefore more clients, the more time and effort you put into making money.

Preparing for What Life Will Throw at You

Bills, jobs, and other responsibilities can throw a lot at us at such a young age. Being prepared for it all will make these surprises a little less scary. Below are some additional things to consider as you navigate early adulthood.

- Insurance: Insurance is a payment made as an agreement where the insurer will cover expenses the insured takes on in case of emergency or on an as-needed basis. You will need insurance for your health, car, apartment, home, and any other property you might own. Insurance helps cover the costs of hospital bills, disasters like floods, or accidents like car accidents or fires at home. Many young adults will be able to stay on their parent's health insurance until they are 25, but if not, make sure you sign up for insurance through healthcare.gov if you are in the U.S. Many apartments will also require that you have renter's insurance, but if not, it's still a good idea to start your own policy.

- Taxes: Taxes are one surefire thing that we have to pay no matter what. If you are working for a company and are hired as an employee, they will likely have you fill out a tax form where you agree to have a certain amount of taxes taken out, usually dependent on your living status (like if you are married or have kids). If not, it's your responsibility to keep track of how much you are making, and set aside 20%-30% of your income to pay quarterly taxes. Then, once taxes are due, it's your responsibility (whether you pay your own taxes or are an employee) to file your yearly income alongside any other expenses you've paid. You can hire someone to do your taxes for you, or utilize a specific website to help you with this process. The most important thing to remember is that even if you only made $1,000 from a small business, like selling repurposed furniture, you will have to pay taxes on that income.

Insurance and taxes are two types of payments that we will never be able to escape. Even if you are incredibly wealthy and have no debt, you will still have to pay these two things in some form. It's best to learn about everything involved so you ensure you are on the right track.

Key Takeaways

Setting yourself up for success involves these strategies:

1. Make the dedication to become financially literate.

2. Understand the way debt grows over time.

3. Find the right job to maintain your income.

4. Utilize methods to grow and expand your income.

5. Prepare for all types of expenditures, like insurance and taxes.

As your knowledge starts to grow, you will gain confidence in your decisions. Learn from your mistakes and do what is best for yourself and your wallet. Take advice from others when they are willing to share, but always remember that everyone's experience is different, and at the end of the day, only you will know what is best for you and your finances.

Chapter 2:

Making the Most of Your Money

Frugality is an important way to ensure you're taking care of your finances. How do you spend your money?

In a week, the average American spends (*Here's How Much*, n.d.):

- $10 on alcohol

- $28 on entertainment

- $64 going out to eat or on takeout

- $80 on groceries

That's $180 a week—or $9,400 a year—on things that *are* important, but are also areas where we could cut corners and reduce expenses. If you could cut out $30 from your grocery, takeout, alcohol, and entertainment budget every week, you would save over $1,500 a year! Chances are, you can spare a penny or two when it comes to your spending habits. What if, instead, you invested that extra $1,500 in something that doubles or triples within a few years?

Life is meant to be enjoyed, so it's important that we give ourselves the freedom to buy food we like and go to concerts or movies with friends. However, by knowing how to stay frugal and penny-pinch when we can, we can maximize the power of our dollar, leading to more opportunities later on in life.

The Power of Saving

Having a little cushion in your finances is a great thing, for obvious reasons. But beyond those, studies show that saving money can actually increase happiness and security in one's life (O'Neill, 2009).

Having a savings account leads to

- more feelings of control.

- a sense of security.

- increased resilience.

It's hard to overcome the urgency or impulsivity that spending money can bring on. When you have the money in your account, and you're at the store or out with friends, resisting the spending triggers that present themselves can feel nearly impossible. However, it is that resiliency that is necessary to help pad your savings.

Savings accounts will help with emergencies and can be used toward bigger purchases in life. When you have money, you have more power over your life. You have the ability to say when and where you choose to spend your money. Not having money, on the other hand, makes it difficult to do the things you want or get the things you deserve. Every time you put a dollar in your savings account, you are doing your future self a favor. Every decision you make to save your money is one that increases your chances of success in the future. A savings account is the most surefire way we can have some semblance of control over what happens in the future.

Money Saving Tips

The best way to set yourself up for success is to open a savings account. A savings account is a separate bank account from your checking and usually isn't associated with checks or debit cards. Having a separate account makes it easier to transfer money over. When that money is sitting in your savings rather than checking, it's easier to follow the motto, "Out of sight, out of mind." If you see $500 extra in your checking, you might start to get some big ideas about how you should spend it.

However, if you move that $500 into savings, you'll then see a smaller amount in your checking, leading you to be less likely to spend it. A savings account can be opened with any major bank. If you already have a checking account, which is a type of bank account typically used for electronic transactions such as withdrawals and deposits, then you can open a savings account with the same bank.

A savings account can sometimes offer compound interest, meaning as your money sits in the account, it will gain more money on top of the initial amount. For example, if you have $1,000 in a savings account with an interest rate of 4.95%, you would have the following:

- $1,024.64 after six months

- $1,051.16 after a year

- $1,269.84 after five years

If you can keep adding more and more, that number will only grow! Below are some important money-saving tips that will help you make the most of your finances:

- Create a budget, and budget for putting money into savings each week or month. I have steps on how to budget in the following section, *Living Within Your Means.*

- Set rules for yourself and stick to them. Examples include not spending money for one week a month (aside from absolute essentials), no purchases of new clothes until you've saved $1,000, or going an entire month without ordering takeout.

- Set monthly goals to follow. This might mean putting $250 in your savings account each month, or putting 10% of each paycheck in the bank. At the end of each month, assess how close you were to reaching your goal, and troubleshoot any major issues that kept you from saving.

Saving is simple. All you have to do is put money into a separate account. It's living within your means and saying *no* to unnecessary purchases that is the hard part!

Living Within Your Means

The best way to live within your means is to first create a budget. A budget is a plan for how you will be spending your finances that you can use to ensure you are only spending as much as you can handle. A budget includes two major parts:

- income

- expenses

Income is anything that you earn, including the following:

- your salary or hourly wage (anything earned on a paycheck)

- money earned from businesses, investments, or rentals

- support from parents, or child support from parents of your children

Expenses include all utilities, bills, and other payments you have to make:

- rent

- mortgage payments

- loan or credit card payments

- electricity

- internet/cable

- water

- sewage

- gas (cooking or heating)

- gas (to drive to and from work/school)

- groceries

- fees or other services (such as streaming services or pet fees)

The first step in budgeting is to list all of your expenses, the amount of each, and the date they are due in chronological order. Here is an example.

Expense	Cost	Date
Rent	$850	1st of the month
Internet	$100	1st of the month
Electricity	$75	1st of the month
Gas	$60	15th of the month
Credit card	$50	20th of the month
Student loans	$200	29th of the month
Streaming service 1	$15	30th of the month
Streaming service 2	$10	30th of the month

As you can see, the total cost of all these expenses is $1,360 a month. After you have your expenses listed, you can then determine if you are making enough money. For this example, let's say someone is making a $600 weekly salary. This means they earn around $2,400 a month. However, after taxes get taken out, that leaves around $1,900 a month.

- $1,900 minus $1,360 leaves a total of $540 per month.

Once you have your leftover income, you can then budget how you will spend that. This leaves around $135 a week. An example budget for this might look like the following:

- $80 on groceries weekly

- $30 for "fun" stuff, like going out with friends or seeing a movie weekly

- $25 for savings weekly

While this is a pretty tight budget, that still leaves some room for fun and for savings. After you lay out your budget, you then have a few options:

- See if there is a way to raise income. Can you take on more hours, ask for a long-deserved raise, or find a part-time gig to give you more money?

- Cut expenses. In this case, you could cut out one or both streaming services to gain more money a month. You could also renegotiate your internet bill to see if there is a cheaper package. Finally, you might consider paying down some of your credit cards with your savings to help lower payments.

Budgeting isn't the easiest thing to do, but once you establish one, you then create a solid foundation for saving money and living within your means.

How to Be More Frugal

Another great way to boost your income and reduce expenses is to live more frugally. Frugality is a mindset or lifestyle where you do as much as you can to save money. The first place to be frugal is with your living situation. Living within your means involves finding an apartment or home that is as low as possible in monthly payments. That means if you're only making $600 a week, you would not want to rent an apartment that is $1,500 a month. Instead, it's best to find a place that would be less than half of what you are currently making.

The next place to be more frugal is with your utility bills. This means unplugging electronics when you aren't using them to lower your electric bill, or keeping the air conditioning and heating as low as possible to reduce other utility costs.

After this, it's important to be frugal when it comes to groceries and shopping. Meal plan ahead of time so you can use as few ingredients as possible. Buy generic brands instead of name brands. Reduce what you use and find ways to recycle or repurpose old things as new. For example, if you have a stain or rip on your jeans, sew on a patch or use dye to change their color—so you have a brand new pair of clothing without having to pay a new sticker price!

If you can find 10 ways to save $5 a month, that boosts your budget by $50! That can make a big difference when you are trying to pay down debt and save your money.

The Biggest Challenges of Saving Money

If saving money were easy, the world would look much different than it does today! Knowing the biggest challenges ahead will help you stay on top of your frugal mindset.

- Impulsivity: Impulses are hard to overcome. Be conscious of marketing tactics that make you feel the need to buy certain things, and don't give into name brands that are unnecessarily expensive. Some name brands are worth the price due to their ethics and quality, but others simply charge for the actual name on the product. Be cognizant of impulsivity in grocery stores, and look out for endcaps and products at the checkout that catch us on our last-minute urges. Always eat before you go grocery shopping to avoid overspending just because you're hungry!

- Unexpected surprises: An emergency fund is the best way to help provide you with a little padding during an emergency, such as an illness or accident that puts you out of work. It never feels great to have to deal with an emergency, but money stress makes it ten times worse. Luckily, emergencies are rare and don't happen frequently, so once you have to spend your emergency fund, you'll hopefully have enough time to build it up again afterward.

- Not having enough to put away: It's hard to save when you don't have enough to actually put away! Look for small gigs to help you earn an extra $20-$100 a month. It might not seem like a lot, but it can make a huge difference. Remember there is no amount that is too small for savings. If all you can do is put $5 in a month, that's still better than $0!

Saving money is a skill that you will get better with over time, so don't be discouraged if you're starting with $0.

Key Takeaways

A dollar holds a certain monetary value, but the actual value of this can be more depending on how you are able to stretch it. Make the most of your money by following these suggestions:

1. Learn the power of saving and create a savings mindset.

2. Look for ways to tighten your budget and cut costs.

3. Take advantage of a frugal mindset to help reuse old items and decrease spending.

4. Know the value of living within your means, and how to say no to things you don't need.

5. Prepare for the biggest challenges of saving money, and do what you can to overcome them.

Saving money isn't the easiest thing to do—if it were, more people wouldn't be struggling with debt. However, once you are able to create a money-saving perspective, you will have what it takes to help your savings expand.

Chapter 3:

A Young Adult's Guide to Good Credit

From credit cards to apartment rentals, there is a lot to learn about what credit is, why it's important to have good credit, and how one can go about obtaining good credit.

Your first credit card can be exhilarating, especially if you open it all on your own without the help of your parents. However, if you're not careful, it can quickly turn stress-inducing and overwhelming. Initially, it can feel as though a credit card is free money. You might get a limit of $300 and be only expected to pay a minimum of $30 a month. Then, before you know it, you're sent offers from other creditors, allowing you to open multiple accounts. When your limit is high, it can feel like the possibilities are endless.

Then something scary can happen. You get a bill letting you know you've reached your limit. On top of that, interest is charged, putting you higher than your limit. You're paying the minimum on four different cards, racking up almost $500 in credit card bills a month, an amount that's almost half your monthly rent.

Credit doesn't seem as exciting when you're still paying off an expensive dress that doesn't even fit you anymore 18 months later!

While credit cards can be very beneficial in many phases of life, they have to be used with care and extensive knowledge to ensure we stay on track.

Credit card debt is at an all-time high. In total, Americans have around $1.079 trillion in credit card debt (Schulz, 2023). This number is alarming, and serves as proof that young adults might be getting themselves in predicaments they weren't anticipating.

What Is Credit?

Credit is important. It is a system of borrowing money where you are granted a large amount up-front, with the promise to make consistent and periodic payments at a specific interest rate. An interest rate is the percentage that is charged on top of the amount initially borrowed. This rate is typically based on the amount of the loan coupled with factors based on your credit history.

There are many different types of credit. The first and most common is a major credit card. These are accounts opened either through your bank or through a major credit card company, like Visa, Mastercard, and American Express. None of these are endorsements, of course, but you might have heard of these companies before. Whatever bank you have a checking account with might also offer you a credit line depending on your qualifications. Major credit cards allow you to spend your money in most places, with some even offering cash withdrawals.

Another type of credit is one taken out through a specific store. Many grocery stores or online stores offer credit cards where you can open a line of credit with the company. For a store card, you can typically only use that card at that specific store, but that varies depending on the company.

Credit also refers to types of loans. I will cover loans in the next chapter.

Having credit is helpful, but only when used responsibly. It's important to maintain a healthy credit score, as this can heavily impact your future.

What Is a Credit Score?

Your credit score is based on your history of taking out and managing credit. Your credit standing could determine your eligibility to borrow money through loans or credit cards, access to housing, and even impact your ability to get a job.

Good credit is important, as it shows lenders that they can trust you. Sometimes credit approval will be determined automatically when applying for smaller loans or credit cards online. Other times, lenders look over your history themselves and will decide that way. This is why no matter what you are applying for, good credit is essential.

Your credit score is determined by many different factors. These can be found on your credit report. A credit report breaks down different aspects of your credit history:

- Amount of credit cards: The type, credit used, and credit available will show up on your credit report. It will also show how long you've had the credit card for.

- Amount and type of loans: All loans, such as student loans, show up on your credit report with the amount listed.

- Inquiries: An inquiry is made on your report when you apply for credit. This will show up even if you apply for something like a credit card but don't get approved. Inquires also show up when certain people check your credit report, like if you apply for an apartment and the property manager runs a credit report.

- Payment history: A credit report shows if you've made payments on time consistently, or if you have missed payments.

- Bankruptcy: If you've filed for bankruptcy, this will show up on your credit report.

Credit reports vary from person to person, and what they include may change over time. For example, medical bills no longer show up on credit reports, though they used to.

The best way to understand whether or not you have good credit is to check your report. If you don't have any credit, that might show a low credit score since you don't have much experience with credit. For that reason, it can be helpful to take out a small credit card when you are young and pay it off immediately. This will show that you are responsible, boosting your credit score over time.

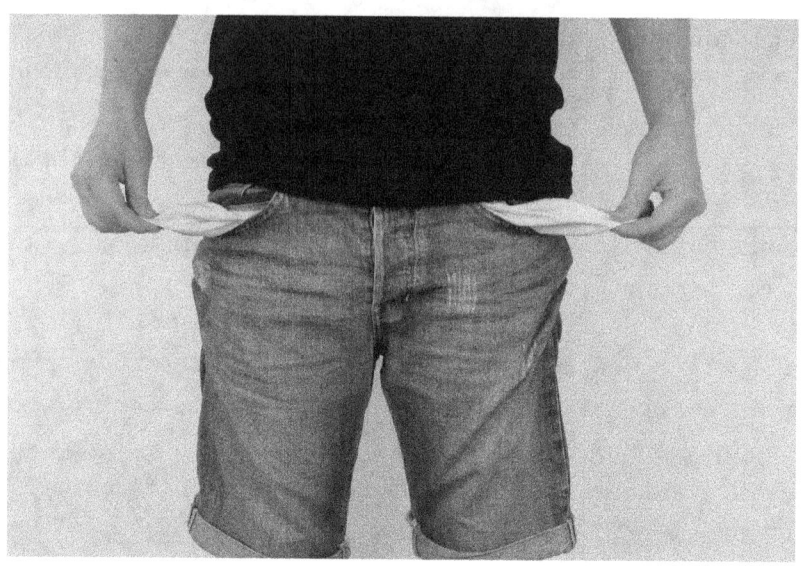

The Limits of Low Credit

There are many different factors that will determine your credit score. You might have low credit if

- you don't have a long history of credit.

- your cards are maxed out or you don't have much credit available.

- you have a long history of missed payments.

A charge-off is also bad for your credit. This occurs when you don't make any payments at all on a credit card. Usually, after your first few payments, you will only be charged a late fee. The credit card company will also likely call you. However, after several months of missed payments and no contact, you will likely be charged off. This closes the credit line and usually involves your debt being sent to a debt collector.

A debt collector is a company that buys large amounts of debt from another larger company, usually for pennies on the dollar. This type of debt collection involves debt that has been ignored for a long period. In some cases of very high credit amounts, a debt agency can actually sue you!

This is why it's always best to communicate, even if you are struggling to make minimum payments. For example, if you lost your job, a major credit card company is likely to work with you by pausing late fees or giving you an extra month to make a payment. This isn't always the case, however, so it's best to stay on top of your payments.

Some loans also involve collateral. This is usually property or other large items that can be collected, or repossessed, by the company if payments are missed. For example, if you don't pay your mortgage, or house loan, you might have your home foreclosed by the bank, forcing you to move out and use the house as collateral for what is still owed. A foreclosure is something else shown on your credit report.

These are extreme cases of failure to pay and situations you should do your best to avoid. Having good credit will make it easier to have higher credit card limits and lower interest rates, making it easier to manage your finances.

Your credit will also determine if you get a certain apartment or job. Some jobs and landlords would rather pick someone with a better credit score, as it might show they are more reliable.

My First Credit Card

Taking out your first credit card can be exciting, but it's important to not let that excitement get to your head. If it does, you might feel tempted to go on a shopping spree or take a luxury vacation. Instead, follow the tips below to help you stay on track:

1. Take out a credit card with a low limit and use it for small purchases that you can pay off right away. For example, if you are going out to lunch with a friend and already have that in your budget, use your credit card and then make a credit card payment later that day. This helps show good credit. You can also take advantage of cash-back rewards from certain credit card companies.

2. Use it to make a larger, strictly necessary purchase, like a bed for your first apartment or a laptop for graduate school. Once you make the big purchase, cut up the credit card and make the largest payments possible.

3. Use less than 1/3 at a time. If you do have to use it for emergencies or to supplement certain purchases, try to keep it under 30% of total use. This will help you maintain a solid credit score.

If you're young and inexperienced, small mistakes aren't a death sentence for your credit history—but keep in mind that many things will stay on your credit report for five years or more. Start small and stay frugal to prevent overspending.

Credit Card Interest Guide

When you get a credit card bill, you will be given a minimum payment that must be made. If not, you might be charged a late fee. Consistently missed minimum payments can impact your credit score. It's essential you make the minimum payment. However, it's encouraged that you make a payment even higher. Only paying off the minimum can mean paying a ton of interest over time.

To help you gain an idea of different interest rates and how they grow over time, use the chart below. This includes a credit card with a specific limit and interest rate, and simulates what would happen if you maxed it out and only paid off the minimum payment.

Credit Limit	Interest Rate (APRs)	Minimum Payment	Months to Pay Off	Amount Paid in Interest After It's Paid Off
$300	26%	$30	18	$216
$1,000	21%	$50	57	$570
$3,000	23.5%	$120	135	$3,150

As you can see, if you only make the minimum payment, it will take a long time to pay off certain debts. When you max out your credit card, you spend a long time paying off a temporary purchase.

Key Takeaways

Credit can be scary to navigate, but it doesn't have to be! While excessive credit card debt is something to avoid, there are times when having credit can be very beneficial to your financial health. Going forward, remember to follow these steps:

1. Familiarize yourself with the different types of credit and what will be best for you.

2. Check your credit score to understand all the types of debt you might have.

3. Look for ways of boosting your credit, like taking out a higher limit and making more frequent and larger payments.

4. Take out a credit card if you don't have one yet, but make sure the limit is small and cut it up to prevent spending it unnecessarily.

5. Identify the amount of interest you have on all of your debt so you can start budgeting for the future.

The ins and outs of credit can be confusing for even the most seasoned financial expert, but don't let it deter you from empowering yourself for the future.

Chapter 4:

The Steps of Making Important Purchases

Now that you have a basic understanding of some of these concepts, it's important to know how to tackle larger purchases.

The average homeowner is 56 years old, with only one in four adults under 25 owning a home (*Homeownership Rate By Age*, 2022). Owning a home is something many of us dream of from a young age. We like to envision what our homes will look like, and who we might be sharing them with.

However, once you start seeing the sticker price, it might feel like a distant dream. Nice houses with many amenities that are in good shape far surpass six digits. When you're only making $25,000 a year, it can feel like owning a home is an impossibility.

I'm here to give you hope that this is not the case! You don't need to have half a million dollars in your bank account to own a home! While homeownership isn't an overnight venture, it is possible to build solid credit, diversify investments, and make yourself look great on paper so that you have what it takes to get a mortgage.

Saving For Down Payments

A down payment is what you put down on a loan before you are granted one. The amount of your down payment will also help with your loan amount, interest rate, or both. This typically means the higher the down payment the better.

How much should your down payment be? It is usually a percentage of a home you are looking for. It's best to start with the average house price in your area. Then, if you have a higher income, you might be able to increase your budget.

A good rule of thumb is to save about 20% of the price of the home you have in mind. For example, if you are looking to purchase a home in your area where the average cost of a home is $250,000, it's best to be prepared with around $50,000. However, you don't always need to have that much, with some loans only requiring 3.5%. This all depends on where you live, your income, and your credit report. Either way, you will likely need at least five digits in savings, so it's best to get started as soon as possible!

Big Purchases

A home is not the only big purchase you will make. Once you buy the home, it might need large appliances, like washers, dryers, and refrigerators. These can often be bought on credit through different stores.

Some homes will also require upgrades. They might need new flooring, a new porch, or a remodeled bathroom. While owning a home is a more lucrative venture than renting in the long run, there are many hidden and unexpected costs to be conscious of as you navigate homeownership.

Auto Loans

Auto loans are loans taken out specifically to pay for automobiles. Cars can be necessary for getting to and from work or school, making them invaluable to some households.

The first thing to know about auto loans is that they can also be taken out through your bank, much like credit cards. However, you don't have to take one out through the bank you currently have. You can find many different options by doing research in your area.

Not all auto loans require down payments, with many offering borrowers cars starting with monthly payments. However, down payments can help reduce your monthly payment.

The loan will have a specific term ranging from 12 months or more. This type of loan is also known as a secure loan, which means that the car will act as collateral. This means if you fail to make payments, the car can be repossessed.

To get approved, you'll need to apply, which will trigger a lender looking at your credit score and income.

Mortgages

Like credit cards and auto loans, mortgages can be taken out through your bank, though there are many lenders to research and consider when making a decision. Since this is such a big purchase, it's crucial to look into multiple different lenders to compare options.

Mortgages require down payments, which is another amount that will vary from person to person. Mortgages are also often much longer-term loans spanning at least a decade, and usually multiple. Monthly payments are then paid, including interest. It's good to have a high credit score to help pay lower interest. In some cases, more interest is paid per month than money on the actual down payment, which can prolong the time it takes to pay off the house. Mortgages are also secured loans, meaning the house will be given to the bank after several failures to pay.

How to Increase Approval Chances

When applying for any type of loan, there are three major things that lenders will review.

- Your credit report: This provides the most comprehensive collection of how much money you've taken out, what debt you have responsibility for, and your history of making on-time payments.

- Your income: You will usually have to prove your income level either by providing pay stubs or records related to your business. A high income shows that you are reliable and that you have the money to make necessary payments. It's also helpful if you've worked at your job for a long time.

- Your debt to income ratio: You might have a high-paying job and good credit, but if you have 10 different credit cards that are all maxed out and thousands of dollars in other loans, it might show that you are a risky lender. It's best to pay off as much debt as possible when preparing for big purchases.

To increase your chances of getting approved, start with your debt. What can be paid down? Can you eliminate a loan or a credit card? Can you split a few thousand dollars across several loans to increase your available credit?

Additionally, it's helpful to show you have good credit. This means if you have no credit at all, it's a good idea to take out a credit card and start building a solid history.

Lastly, look for ways to increase your income. Married couples can sometimes have better approval chances, so consider if you and your partner might want to make this purchase together. If you are buying a home on your own, consider adding an additional income stream. Eventually you might be able to phase this out, but it can be a temporary way to save money and improve your approval chances.

Key Takeaways

What the future holds is excitement, new opportunities, and the fulfillment of all of our greatest dreams. But to get there, we must ensure we know how to save for important purchases! Below are the next steps to take to empower yourself and your financial future:

1. Start saving specifically for a down payment on your house; you won't regret putting this money aside!

2. Know everything involved with making a big purchase, and create a checklist so you know what you will or won't need to get approved.

3. Familiarize yourself with auto loans if you are planning on getting a car, or check over the one you currently have to determine what you have left to pay.

4. Familiarize yourself with mortgages, and consider what you might get preapproved for based on your income and potential down payment.

5. Troubleshoot your credit and income to see how you can boost your chances of getting approved.

The future is not as far ahead as it seems, so take the necessary steps to prepare now!

Chapter 5:

Money Managing Mindset

Sometimes it's not about how much money or credit we have, but instead, the mindset we have around money. Over three in four Americans are anxious about their current financial situation (White, 2023). Can you blame them? When we don't have enough money, all we think about is how we're going to pay our bills and get ahead. When we do have money, we worry about what we're going to do with it. When we figure out what to do with our money in a smart way, we start to worry that suddenly, we'll lose everything we worked so hard for.

It seems like there is never enough money to satisfy us and make us happy. The more we have, the more we want, and the more we want, the harder we have to work. The harder we work, the more we have to lose, and this risk can stress us out!

While financial literacy is essential, what's more important is that we know how to live and enjoy our lives while we are still here to do so! Bills will always linger, and there's no escaping taxes. Embracing financial freedom also means recognizing that it's okay to have to pay bills. It's okay to have some debt, and it's okay to not have as much money as we'd like. That doesn't mean we can't still enjoy life in the process.

Emergency Funds

Emergency funds are portions of money set aside specifically for emergencies. These can be specific accounts, like a long-term savings account. Some people also have credit cards specifically for emergencies. Either way, it's best to ensure that you allocate funds for an emergency. You might find that you have lost your job and need some additional income to supplement funds for a temporary period. Emergencies might be health-related, or based on a natural disaster, like a hurricane or even a global pandemic. While it's good to hope that you never need to use one, you don't want to have to go without an emergency fund when it actually is necessary.

Investments

Investments are something to consider as a means to help your business grow. These are some investment examples:

- stocks

- options

- bonds

- exchange-traded funds

These typically involve putting money into specific companies or banks that carry a certain risk. While you're young is a great time to invest as you likely have less responsibility, and therefore more freedom to take risks. However, when you're inexperienced, that can also make you the most vulnerable.

It's best to diversify your investments. This means picking more than one to put money into rather than making a bet on a large investment. Investments shouldn't be a gamble where you put money in that you couldn't afford to lose. Stay smart with investing and go with your gut to keep your money safe.

Overcoming Money Stress

Money is a source of stress. It can be very overwhelming to know how to manage your money in the best way possible. One thing you might struggle with is a scarcity mindset. This involves feeling as though you don't have as much as you do, or intense feelings of urgently needing more. Scarcity mindsets can be very damaging to our finances. For example, if you are desperate to make money, you might be more likely to take a big risk, like gambling what you do have. You might also stress over purchases and deal with intense buyer's remorse. To help keep money stress at bay, follow these tips.

- Keep strong records: Always write down what you are making and spending so you never deal with surprise purchases.

- Don't give in to feelings of urgency and impulses. Take 24 hours, at the minimum, to think over all purchases, including small purchases like ordering takeout. Rather than making an impulsive purchase, instead plan a time ahead in the future to reward yourself for financial responsibility.

- Commit to saving: Like brushing your teeth or doing the dishes, think of saving as something you simply *have* to do. Even if it only means putting away $1 a week, make it a habit of transferring money into savings to help you make the most of your finances.

At the end of the day, remember that money only provides temporary relief; it is not the key to happiness. It reduces stress, but not having money doesn't mean you can't still be happy.

One thing that might get in your way going forward is a materialist mindset. This involves feeling as though big purchases and fancy items will provide you with status, identity, and happiness. Make sure to foster awareness of how you are spending money in relation to how that makes you feel. Are you happy with your items, and would you still buy them without the social pressure surrounding them? Know the difference between what you *need* and what you *want*.

Coming Back After Financial Setbacks

Everyone makes mistakes, and that means we all make some when it comes to money as well! Sometimes you might take a risk that simply doesn't pay off. That does not mean you are doomed forever! When you find yourself facing a financial setback, focus on repaying what you can and building up your savings once again.

At the end of the day, it's important to contact a professional when you are uncertain of what to do. It's better to spend a little money getting advice, than to lose money from making a poor financial decision. Mistakes are chances for us to learn and grow—all an important part of becoming a responsible young adult!

Key Takeaways

Money can be the root of some of life's biggest stressors. When this happens, it is distracting and takes away from our ability to enjoy life around us. To help you stay in the right headspace to make the most of your finances, follow these steps:

1. Set aside money in an emergency fund so you feel prepared for whatever lies ahead.

2. Start investing some of your savings, no matter how small, to help your money grow.

3. Remind yourself that it takes time to save money, and just because you feel like you don't have enough now doesn't mean things will stay that way forever.

4. Self-reflect to see if you have some materialist tendencies, and do what you can to reduce them to stay focused on what's most important.

5. Know that you will make some mistakes and run into some setbacks, but these will be learning experiences that propel you forward.

At the end of the day, what we go through on our own is an individual experience that can either become a powerful learning opportunity or the start of many more mistakes. You decide what path you will be taking going forward, so do what you can to set yourself up for success in the best way possible.

Conclusion

Many of life's greatest lessons are learned through our mistakes. No one is perfect, so take a moment to remind yourself that no matter what has happened in your financial life so far, you have plenty of life ahead of you to change things for the better.

There are many young people who struggle with regret. They regret not saving more. They regret spending so much on their education. They regret *not* spending more on their education and gaining a college experience.

I'm here to remind you that going forward, every experience you've lived through is one that shapes our future. There's no way of knowing what lies ahead, which means there's also no knowing what would have happened had we made different decisions. Perhaps things would be better had we saved more, but maybe not! Things could have just as easily gone worse, so all we can do is accept the past for what it is, and do our best to move toward a brighter and more empowering future.

As we finish up, I want to provide you with one last action plan so you know exactly what steps to take next:

1. Study your finances! This guide was a brief overview of some of the most important things to know. There are books on just taxes or credit card interest with hundreds of pages, so there is plenty to know about finances. Even though you might think you know it all, never stop learning about how you can make your money grow.

2. Live within your means. This is the most important monetary rule that I wish more people knew. If you know how to say no to unnecessary purchases and avoid impulsive decisions, you will be able to save your money for the things that are most important in life.

3. Become a credit connoisseur. Get to know the ins and outs of different types of credit so you are aware of what you will need going forward. Once you do take out a credit card, be careful to stay within the limit and focus on making maximum payments, not minimum ones.

4. Prepare for big purchases. Set aside money for down payments and always review your checklist for getting approved for auto or home loans. Becoming a homeowner is not something that is a distant fantasy! It can happen sooner than you'd expect.

5. Remember to keep the right mindset. Those without a ton of money are able to expand it into a fortune, and those with a fortune are able to burn through their money and quickly lose it all. It's not about how much you have to work with, but how you choose to work with it that matters most.

If you liked what you've read in this guide, start a conversation and leave a review! Let me know what you liked the most, and what more you'd like for future books!

The future is unknown and finances can be scary. Combined, this can be enough to cause us to panic, but don't worry. You have the tools you need to get started toward a more powerful future, so now it's time to use them!

Glossary

- **Asset:** Something of value owned by a company or individual, usually cash, property, equipment, or investments. Assets can typically be liquidated into cash.

- **Budget:** A financial plan used as a means to track income and expenses to balance money over a specific period of time.

- **Checking account:** A type of bank account typically used for electronic transactions such as withdrawals and deposits. Checking accounts often have debit cards which allow for quick transactions.

- **Credit:** This refers to the act of borrowing money with an expectation of repayment in the future, usually granted to businesses or individuals.

- **Credit report:** A detailed history of an individual's credit such as loans, credit cards, payment history, and other important financial information. This is typically used by businesses to assess whether credit will be given to an inquiring borrower.

- **Credit score:** A measure of an individual's creditworthiness, based on factors like credit amount, payment reliability, and other important financial information.

- **Debt:** Debt is any money owed with an expectation of repayment, such as money taken out as a loan or purchases made using a credit card.

- **Diversification:** This is a process of spreading investments out across multiple different methods to reduce the risk of money lost.

- **Down payment:** Money that is paid toward the total cost of a purchase, or money paid upfront to show good credit.

- **Emergency fund:** A savings account filled specifically for emergencies, disasters, or accidents to cover unexpected costs.

- **Expense:** A cost for goods or services, either that has already been paid or is expected to be paid through a budget.

- **Frugal:** The act of limited and thrifty spending to reduce costs and expenses in order to save money or make it last longer than expected.

- **Income:** Any money that is earned or paid to an individual or business, like salaries, wages, investments, or other funds.

- **Insurance:** An agreement between a business or individual with another business or entity to cover certain costs, usually maintained with regular payments, such as health or car insurance.

- **Interest:** A percentage charged on debts or investments, like loans or savings accounts, that is expected to be paid on top of initial debts or earned on top of the initial investment. This is usually a set amount and is based on a number of factors.

- **Investment:** A type of money or resource spent on an asset or project with the expectation of additional income generation over time.

- **Internal Revenue Service (IRS):** The government agency responsible for maintaining, charging, and enforcing federal taxes in the United States.

- **Loan:** A financial agreement between two entities where the borrower receives money with the expectation to pay it back to the lender over a period of time, usually with interest charged on top of the initial amount in addition to set fees.

- **Materialism:** A mindset focused on material possession, wealth, and consumerism whereas the acquisition of these materials usually results in a perceived boost in happiness.

- **Mortgage:** A real estate loan used for the purchase of houses or property, with similar expectations of other loans like fees, down payments, and interest.

- **Move-in fee:** A one-time payment charged before renters move into a rental property, charged by property managers or landlords. The costs are typically used for expenses related to moving.

- **Rent:** Any type of payment made on a property by a lender to a landlord or property manager for both commercial and residential properties, usually paid on a recurring basis.

- **Savings account:** Money that is set aside in a specific account for various reasons, such as emergencies, investments, or other specific purposes.

- **Scarcity mindset:** A mindset or belief system where the individual feels excessive fear over not having enough, which can sometimes lead to impulsivity or poor decision-making skills.

- **Security deposit:** A refundable amount of money paid at the start of a financial agreement, usually for lenders or landlords paid by the lender or tenant.

References

Financial literacy for youth: Why it matters. (2023, June 6). United Way. https://unitedwaynca.org/blog/financial-literacy-for-youth/

Hanson, M. (2023, May 22). *Average student loan debt.* Education Data. https://educationdata.org/average-student-loan-debt

Here's how much the average American spends in a day—how do you measure up? (n.d.). Sunmark. https://www.sunmark.org/connect/sunmark-360/heres-how-much-average-american-spends-day-how-do-you-measure

Homeownership rate by age. (2022, October 1). Property Management. https://ipropertymanagement.com/research/homeownership-rate-by-age

O'Neill, B. (2009, February). *The benefits of saving money.* Rutgers. https://njaes.rutgers.edu/sshw/message/message.php?p=Finance&m=122

Payne, K. (2023, September 18). *Average American savings account balance.* Time. https://time.com/personal-finance/article/average-american-savings-account-balance/

Renter, E. (2023, May 9). *Most Americans save, but many can't cover $1,000 emergency.* Nerd Wallet. https://www.nerdwallet.com/article/banking/data-2023-savings-report

Schulz, M. (2023, December 14). *2024 credit card debt statistics.* Lending Tree. https://www.lendingtree.com/credit-cards/credit-card-debt-statistics/

Study: Parents are the biggest financial influence for 1 in 3 young adults. (2023, January 31). The Zebra. https://www.thezebra.com/resources/research/financial-independence-report/

Turner, T. (2023, December 7). *47+ fascinating financial literacy statistics in 2023.* Annuity. https://www.annuity.org/financial-literacy/financial-literacy-statistics/

White, A. (2023, November 9). *77% of Americans are anxious about their financial situation—here's how to take control.* CNBC. https://www.cnbc.com/select/how-to-take-control-of-your-finances/

Image References

Alisadyson. (2022, June 12). *Family, African-American, happy*. [Image]. Pixabay. https://pixabay.com/photos/family-african-american-happy-7257182/

Anncapictures. (2018, July 13). *Financing, housebuilding, to build*. [Image]. Pixabay. https://pixabay.com/photos/financing-housebuilding-to-build-3536755/

Borevina. (2019, January 24). *Beautiful people, beauty, blond hair*. [Image]. Pixabay. https://pixabay.com/photos/beautiful-people-beauty-blond-hair-3954533/

ccfb. (2020, February 18). *Finance, bank, banking*. [Image]. Pixabay. https://pixabay.com/photos/finance-bank-banking-business-4858797/

Clarkdonald413. (2019, June 7). *Dog, pet, nature*. [Image]. Pixabay. https://pixabay.com/photos/dog-pet-canine-animal-walking-4259565/

Firmbee. (2015, January 28). *Bookkeeping, accounting, taxes*. [Image]. Pixabay. https://pixabay.com/photos/bookkeeping-accounting-taxes-615384/

Foundry. (2015, August 2). *African American, computer, technology*. [Image]. Pixabay. https://pixabay.com/photos/african-american-computer-technology-869673/

Goumbik. (2018, March 11). MONEY, WALLET, FINANCE. [Image]. Pixabay. https://pixabay.com/photos/money-wallet-finance-cash-business-3219337/

Maklay62. (2016, May 31). *Money, dollars, success*. [Image]. Pixabay. https://pixabay.com/photos/money-dollars-success-business-1428594/

Nattanan23. (2017, September 6). *Money, coin, investment*. [Image]. Pixabay. https://pixabay.com/photos/money-coin-investment-business-2724241/

Nosheep. (2016, December 5). *Money, savings, piggy*. [Image]. Pixabay. https://pixabay.com/photos/money-savings-piggy-white-1885540/

Paulbr75. (2016, July 26). *New home, for sale, luxury*. [Image]. Pixabay. https://pixabay.com/photos/new-home-for-sale-luxury-house-1540871/

RoboAdvisor. (2019, October 1). *Money back up, save money, save up*. [Image]. Pixabay. https://pixabay.com/photos/money-back-up-save-money-save-up-4518407/

Schuldnerhilfe. (2016, June 6). *Pockets, empty, jeans*. [Image]. Pixabay. https://pixabay.com/photos/pockets-empty-jeans-no-money-1439412/

777546. (2015, May 12). *Accounting, report, credit card*. [Image]. Pixabay. https://pixabay.com/photos/accounting-report-credit-card-761599/

Shutterbug75. (2016, March 4). *Agree, agreement, asian*. [Image]. Pixabay. https://pixabay.com/photos/agree-agreement-asian-black-1238964/

Stevepb. (2014, July 8). *Calculator, calculation, insurance*. [Image]. Pixabay. https://pixabay.com/photos/calculator-calculation-insurance-385506/

TBIT. (2015, September 15). *Bank notes, dollar, us dollars*. [Image]. Pixabay. https://pixabay.com/photos/bank-notes-dollar-us-dollars-usd-941246/

TheDigitalWay. (2016, August 10). *Credit cards, denim, jeans*. [Image]. Pixabay. https://pixabay.com/photos/credit-cards-denim-jeans-blue-jeans-1583534/

089photoshootings. (2017, January 14). *Woman, man, kitchen*. [Image]. Pixabay. https://pixabay.com/photos/woman-man-kitchen-food-preparation-1979272/

www.ingramcontent.com/pod-product-compliance
Lightning Source LLC
Chambersburg PA
CBHW081002290526
45795CB00009B/3047